My Visions,
My Truths

Poems
& Inspirations

by J.M. Sinatra Mac Neil

MFB
<<<>>>
Buffalo, NY

ISBN: 978-0692437001
Mac Neil, Jennifer M. Sinatra/My Visions, My Truths: Poems & Inpirations-2nd ed.

1. Poems. 2. Healing. 3. Personal growth.

4. Self-development. 5. Inspiration 6. Spiritual

1. Mac Neil. 2. Verse

Photographs were taken by the author in and around Buffalo, NY.

No Frills Buffalo/Amelia Press
<<<>>>
119 Dorchester Road
Buffalo, New York 14213
For more information please visit
nofrillsbuffalo.com

GOD,

Thank you for bringing me through this adversity and realization; "Challenges do make you stronger." I am forever grateful for my husband Dylan. My most precious gift from you.

Contents

Previously Published Poems

My Visions,
My Truths

Poems & Inspirations

Introduction

A journey that had to be made, and I reluctantly picked up the pen and began to write. Fixated on the chronic pain and path of suffering, I refused to let the light back in. The light that once filled me was nowhere to be found.

I was aware of what was expected of me. To submit. Yes, submit my life to God. No more questions. No more nit-picking or resistance. I had to remove all obstacles. How did I end up here after working for so long on my light? How did my desire to help others get taken away? No more volunteering. No more working. It was just me and these stupid, all too white, walls.

I thought this daily.

Was this the end for me? Was I searching an empty mind, or one filled with resentment and hate? I needed to submit. I often found myself staring into space, screaming at God above, burying my head in a pillow, or numbly watching pointless television. I wanted to escape the situation I was in. Would the combination of pain, LUPUS, Rheumatoid Arthritis (RA) and various other aliments be my end?

No.

I prayed. I went to physical therapy exercise and acupuncture. I saw minute improvements. Time passed, and I was impatient.

"Oh Lord," I cried out,

"I'm only forty-one. Get me out of here."

"What do I need to do?"

"Help me. Please, help me."

More time passed.

Then, rhymes and verses starting coming into my head. I tried to block them out, but they persisted. I started to write them down. This flow kept coming, and I continued writing. I was writing poetry! I had written poetry back in the nineteen-nineties but somehow got away from it. Now, I was doing it unconsciously – it was…automatic. My creative juices were flowing again.

My Visions, My Truths is the result. It is a book of poems and photographs which expresses my feelings and the situation I was in. These poems demonstrate how I am seeing my way through it.

I learned that we all need to work together, to encourage each other, to find our own moments of happiness.

Honestly, my best days were at home with God praying and searching my soul. I truly believe He answers us all if we give Him a chance to be heard.

Look within – in silence.

There you will find, where your best journey begins.

Life

My mind is troubled...

My motivation is none...

Can't think straight

Not even one song

Very sleepy all the time

Restlessness

Not calm with itchiness all over

Chest beating so fast it hurts

So uncomfortable in my own skin and in life

Do I care? Of course I do

But,

What do I do...

Next?

My Light

Flash of night

Light so bright

My first night with you tonight

Doves surround me

Wild horses run 'long side

I reach for you

I accept you

You are my destiny

Will you accept me?

Yes,

       You do.

Freeness of One's Mind

As I sit by the water
Nothing comes to mind
As I sit by the water
      Not a cloud in the sky
The earth is so perfect
      The waves so sublime
The sun glares on the water
      With no end in sight
The breeze of fresh air touches my face
      Wind dancing in my hair
Me crouched on a rock
      Watching seagulls pass by

This particular day was long and hard
      Frustrated and overwhelmed
      Again nothing comes to mind
      Staring at the lake
I take a breath, looking to my left
      Nothing comes to mind
I look at the ground…
I look to my right…
      Again not a cloud in the sky
Nothing comes to mind
It is a freeness of my mind
A Freeness of One's Mind.

Fulfilled

Amazingly, my muse is water
Lakes, rivers, or oceans
My head doesn't wander
My heart is so fulfilled
I do not worry about people
I am not worrying about the bills
I am not worrying about having children
Or worried about the pain
I'm usually filled with.

Amazingly,
      Life is so simple here
      Life is so tranquil
      Life is never ending
      Hope is fulfilled
I do not worry about people,
      Work, or the bills
I am not worrying about tomorrow
Or my health and this
      Uphill battle

My heart is fulfilled
The waves hitting the rocks
Waves hitting the shore
Waves hitting each other
Reflections of the water
The future is so clear...
My heart is fulfilled.

My Mother's Game

Thinking of my mother since she passed away
Remembering her most favorite game
Numbers being called- One by one
Caller standing on cue
      All but one thing to do
Players dot, dot, dot
      Only dabbing a few numbers at a time
Frustratons and anticipation getting higher
Only the prize in mind, time for
Coverall- not my number again
People are antsy in their seats
      And start to vent
Only eight numbers left
NOW will I get the last three?
Praying begins "Lord, help me now"
Disappointment fills the air...
      Sighs from everyone, except one
Bingo was called, not me this time
Let's try again.

Blessings

Taking a deep breath
Knowing blessings will be revealed
My Lord, my savior is always near
Troubles on my mind
Some small, some large
Blessings are here
No troubles fill my mind.

The Unknown

Time goes by
Troubles subside
Time goes by
I can't make up my mind
Which path should I take?
How do I decide?
Everything is so new,
What do I do..?

Change

Whispers

       Lies

            Heartbreak

No surprise!

      Change

           Must happen

                Time

                      Never dies...

Not Complicated

Life isn't as complicated as it seems
Days go by
Flashes like dreams
Smiles
Children and sweet, sweet sounds
All part of this wonderful dream
Crisp, frequent sounds from the wind
Echoes like dreams of a band
     With strings
Beat, beat, beat
     Go the drums.

My Ladybug

I cried knowing the end could be here
>Will I be alright?

So much uncertainty

So much unknown, nothing in sight

My last hope, my last breath?

I cried out to God,

"Will I be alright?
>Please send me a sign"

I laid my head down on my pillow for
>Possibly one last night

Morning came and I would soon know my fate

I notice something fall off my cell phone
>And down to the ground

A wonderful sigh of relief as

I pick it up and laid it in my open palm

He answered me – My Ladybug
>A ladybug was in the palm of my hand.

>I cried in delight,

"Thank you God, I will be alright!"

Realization of Self

Calmness fills the air
Forgiveness is all around
My spirit is ready to fly
And I'm
Almost settled down.

Scared

I'm so scared
So separated from the world
I know it will be alright
I know I will be whole again
Still
      I'm scared.

Deep

It's times like this
Times of hardship and strife
  To realize one's character
  One's one-ness
Buried deep inside
How deep are you?
Or do you not know since you've been
Burying everything for so long?
Is it time to dig yourself
Out of the canyon you've created?
  Just remember, it didn't happen overnight
  Give yourself time to find YOU all over again
Better yet—the New You!

Beating

My heart beats fast everyday
Excitement is all around
Changes are coming my way
      Lots of change
Will anyone pay attention?
Will anyone hear a sound?
My heart beats faster every day.

Traveling

My travel continues
As my mind continues to race
What is my destiny?
Where is my fate?
So many challenges ahead –
All I will face
Times are growing stronger.

As my future becomes more clear
The paths I must take
The choices I will make
Fold up evenly and straight
To be the few
The one
    I do not understand, how
    I will persevere, how
    I will be strong, how
    I will heal.
    I will, through Him;
Make the Difference
Through Him, I've won!

Happiness

Thoughts of happiness
Fleeting at times
People's despair all around
Seeking happiness
Seeking revenge
What do people want?
Do they really care?
How do you know?
How will *I* know?

Healing

How could they be real?
Could my dreams be true?
An unknown woman with long white hair
Seeking God's protection
Looking for God's touch
Cancer fills her body unknowingly
It's just a matter of time
Prayers shout out every day
No-one knows her fate
Amazingly, she wakes up another day.

:-)

Attacks

Attack, attack, attack
      One, two, three
Will he ever let me be?
Knocking me down, day by day
Watching me fall to my knees
What is going on here?
Why is this happening to me?
He stands in my way at
      Every turn, every move
The pain is real; the pain is difficult to bear
What do I do? How do I make it through?
I am losing this fight
What do I do? How do I begin?

My heart beats faster

My heart is closer to the ground

Down on my knees

Will he win?

At my end, not knowing

Where to go, where to proceed

Then I call out

Through talks with friends and reading scriptures

I begin to heal, through fellowship and His word -

Finally my true path appears.

My Gift

A mate, so strong and true
A gift from God
Who chooses to always be by my side
Together we travel down life's path as one
And though, many times we've struggled
Throughout this life's journey
We continue down the road.

Still problems arise again but with
Quick fixes or permanent repairs
We continue down the road
Together facing adversity, loss, and disappointment

Down this road, traveling as one;
Is life's true gift.

Devil's Delight

Hold tight to the thoughts and wisdom

Of your spiritual guides' proven ways

Indulgences, like sugars and sweets

Rob you of God's given treats like the sun and rain

Know that prayers will guide you

Away from the devil's delights

Your spirit will soar and you

Will finally take flight

Psalms and praise are Gods given ways!

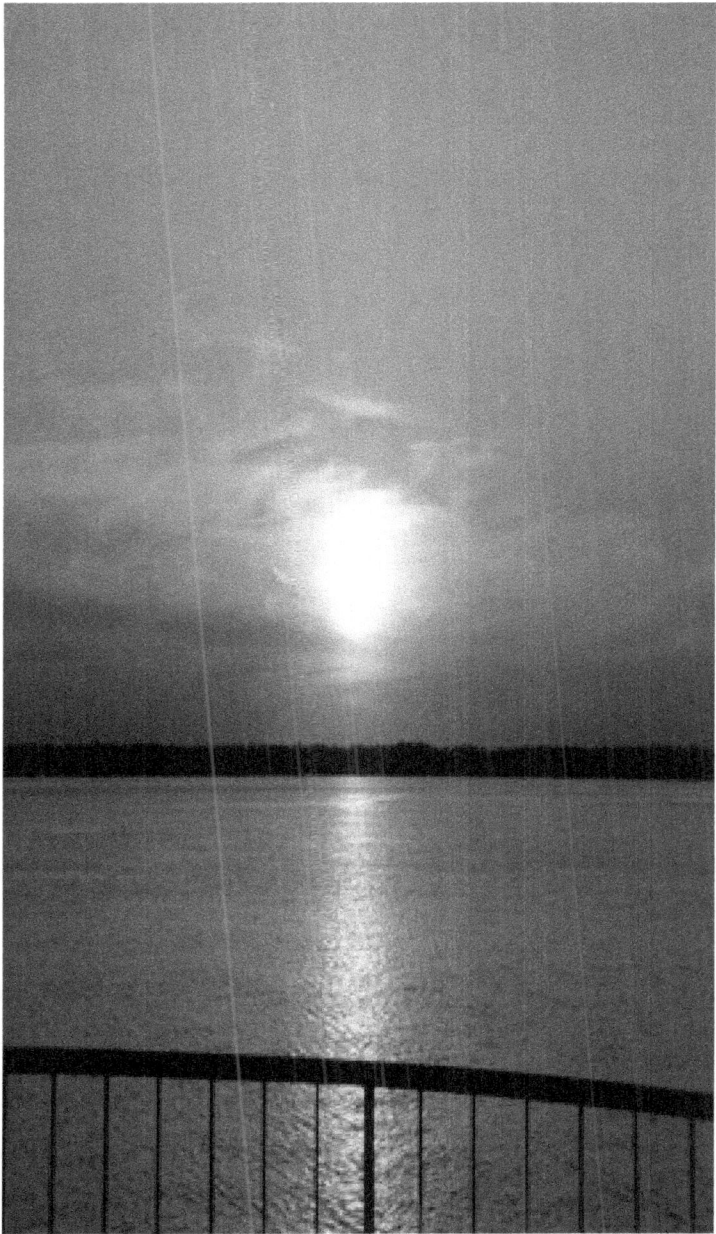

Sleep

Time to sleep and rest

For your body and mind to create its' safety net

Space to rejuvenate

A state of hypnotic bliss

Which we all enjoy

To gently be able to remove the stresses of life

     Or indiscretions

Are they removed, are they ever truly gone?

     Breathe in

     Breathe out

And leave your sadness and worries behind

Sleep my friend; sleep

     Tomorrow is a brand new, fabulous

Wonderful day.

To Grow

Our parents guide us the best they know how
Hopefully each generation is better than the next
Although we may skip a generation, we grow
Just know, you are never alone
God brings us through adversity
Time and time again

Don't put limits on yourself
Know when to leave
So you too can continue to grow
Our parents guide us the best they know how
So we choose, if we continue to grow...
Do you want to grow?
Are you growing?

I think it's time to grow.

A Mother's Inspiration

Does a mother ever leave?
Whether alive or dead
Her impact lingers
Whether good or bad, the child can't distinguish
If what they learned
Should be used or discarded.

Another trial and error episode continues
Will the cycle end with you
Or continue to the next generation?
A goal for all,
To become better than the generation before
To learn something and pass it on
So encourage, I say. Learn, I say.
         And then teach with confidence
Pass that on, I say.

Road to Discovery

Amazing how people tell you what you need

To be bigger and better

Faster and stronger

Happier and healthier. But simply

It is:

> To choose life and living;

> To choose hope and dreaming;

> To turn the other cheek

> To always discover

And to always Love.

The road to discovery is manifested

When you don't let other

People's ideas cloud your own

> -When letting go of everyday norms

And other people's perceptions are a must

> -Find your Roar

> -Find You!

Dreamy Thoughts

Embrace life

Don't

Waste it!

A Moment

Life is just fleeting moments

Life is created unknowingly

Life is spared

Life is missed

Life is created again

Life is in the moment

A moment

Life is today.

See

See through the negativity

    The hate and the jealousy

See through the pain one has

    Inflicted on thee

See the child inside,

    Allow them to shine

See colors so bright

Your colors, which may have dimmed from sight

Just believe –

Open your eyes and –

Just See.

Stand

Stand your ground
Though shaky at times
Stand your ground
Your troubles will soon fade away, because
Tomorrow is always a better day
Stand your ground.

Be proud of who you are
With knicks, scrapes and scars,
Weathered and worn
Stand your ground
Be True— To You
        And
        - Stand.

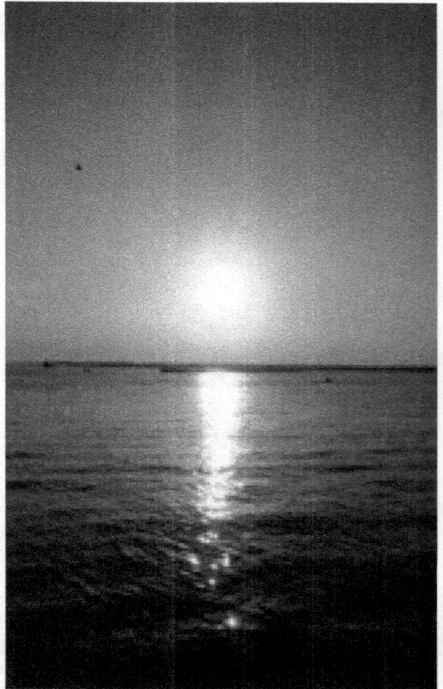

Miracle Way

Traveling yet another day

To find that street called "Miracle Way"

Knocking on every door

Walking miles to find

One ounce of a better day

No one knows my pain

No one cares of my sorrow

Yet I continue to

Travel toward my better day

Because I will, find my "Miracle Way".

My Understanding

Why is this happening?

People are so cruel

Even vicious at times

No harmony or understanding

No rhythm, no rhyme

The beats in my heart grow silent

The music in my head is never heard

I know when I turn that corner

My life will no longer seem absurd

My Visions, My Truths…

Will finally be heard!

My First Poem into
The National Library of Poetry.
(2/97)

Bowling is Just Like Men

Bowling is just like men
You can never control it
You can never figure it out
And
When you finally think everything
Is going right
You split-
Up.

My Second Poem into
The National Library of Poetry.
(3/99)

Once in a While - Patience

Once in a while things do go wrong...
This turns life into a sad, sad, song...
But with patience Amen…
You will see my heart is true
And no matter how much we argue
You will always be able to tell
I Forever Love You!!!

About the Author

Jennifer Sinatra MacNeil was born in Buffalo, New York in 1969. Her childhood was spent on the West Side of Buffalo, a diverse and impoverished area. Her Mother, Marie, was a home maker. She passed at the age of 51. Her father Sam, was a truck driver for the Buffalo News-Sunrise edition. He passed at the age of 45. Her father often shared his spiritual passion for God with Jennifer and this would help her later on in life.

Ms. MacNeil attended High School and college in Buffalo. She obtained a dual Bachelor of Arts in Math/Computer Science and Philosophy from D'Youville College. Dr. Robert Nielsen was quite influential in her college years, making her contemplate life and her existence in this life. One of his most used references was from a song by Peggy Lee; "Is that all there is?"

Since the age thirteen, she has volunteered her time helping others. For her first volunteer position, she worked the summer away at Deaconess Hospital; working five days a week. Jennifer purged folders and visited patients on the floors of the Hospital. This experience shaped her future, as she would continue to volunteer and help Buffalo's surrounding communities. She worked in the administrative field for the Federal Government for almost 20 years; until a work injury disabled her. Jennifer has received numerous community and work awards, certificates and recognitions.

Ms. MacNeil enjoys being a wife and world travel. She also loves animals, nature, and singing in her church choir. Jennifer's biggest passion lies with a disease she was stricken with at the age of 19; LUPUS. She is a Lupus advocate, and enjoys reaching out to others through social media and by fundraising for the local Lupus Alliance of Upstate New York.